ReadyGEN
Text Colle

MW00655569

SAVVAS
LEARNING COMPANY

ISBN-13: 978-0-328-85794-4
ISBN-10:   0-328-85794-7

11 20

Understanding Then and Now

THE LITTLE HOUSE

HER STORY

BY

VIRGINIA LEE BURTON

THE CALDECOTT MEDAL

4

Once upon
a time there
was a Little House
way out in the country.
She was a pretty Little House
and she was strong and well built.
The man who built her so well said,
"This Little House shall
never be sold for gold or silver
and she will live to see our
great-great-grandchildren's
great-great-grandchildren
living in her."

5

The Little House was very happy as she sat
on the hill and watched the countryside around her.
She watched the sun rise in the morning
and she watched the sun set in the evening.
Day followed day,
each one a little different from the one before . . .
but the Little House stayed just the same.

In the nights she watched the moon grow
from a thin new moon to a full moon, then back again
to a thin old moon; and when there was no moon
she watched the stars. Way off in the distance
she could see the lights of the city.
The Little House was curious about the city
and wondered what it would be like to live there.

7

Time passed quickly for the Little House as she
watched the countryside slowly change with the seasons.
In the Spring, when the days grew longer and
the sun warmer, she waited for the first robin to return
from the South. She watched the grass turn green.
She watched the buds on the trees swell
and the apple trees burst into blossom.
She watched the children playing in the brook.

8

In the long Summer days she sat in the sun
and watched the trees cover themselves
with leaves and the white daisies cover the hill.
She watched the gardens grow,
and she watched the apples turn red and ripen.
She watched the children swimming in the pool.

9

In the Fall, when the days grew shorter
and the nights colder,
she watched the first frost turn the leaves
to bright yellow and orange and red.
She watched the harvest gathered and the apples picked.
She watched the children going back to school.

In the Winter, when the nights were long and the days
short, and the countryside covered with snow,
she watched the children coasting and skating.
Year followed year. . . .
The apple trees grew old and new ones were planted.
The children grew up and went away to the city . . .
and now at night the lights of the city
seemed brighter and closer.

11

One day the Little House was surprised to see a horseless
carriage coming down the winding country road. . . .
Pretty soon there were more of them on the road and fewer
carriages pulled by horses. Pretty soon along came some
surveyors and surveyed a line in front of the Little House.
Pretty soon along came a steam shovel and dug a road
through the hill covered with daisies. . . .
Then some trucks came and dumped big stones on the road,
then some trucks with little stones, then some trucks with tar
and sand, and finally a steam roller came and rolled it
all smooth, and the road was done.

Now the Little House watched
the trucks and automobiles
going back and forth to the city.
Gasoline stations . . .
roadside stands . . .
and small houses followed the new road.
Everyone and everything
moved much faster now than before.

13

More roads were made,
and the countryside was divided into lots.
More houses and bigger houses . . .
apartment houses and tenement houses . . .
schools . . . stores . . . and garages
spread over the land
and crowded around the Little House.
No one wanted to live in her and take care
of her any more. She couldn't be sold for gold or silver,
so she just stayed there and watched.

Now it was not so quiet and peaceful at night.
Now the lights of the city were bright and very close,
and the street lights shone all night.
"This must be living in the city," thought the Little House,
and didn't know whether she liked it or not.
She missed the field of daisies
and the apple trees dancing in the moonlight.

15

Pretty soon there were trolley cars
going back and forth in front of the Little House.
They went back and forth all day
and part of the night.
Everyone seemed to be very busy
and everyone seemed to be in a hurry.

16

Pretty soon there was an elevated train
going back and forth above the Little House.
The air was filled with dust and smoke,
and the noise was so loud
that it shook the Little House.
Now she couldn't tell when Spring came,
or Summer or Fall, or Winter.
It all seemed about the same.

17

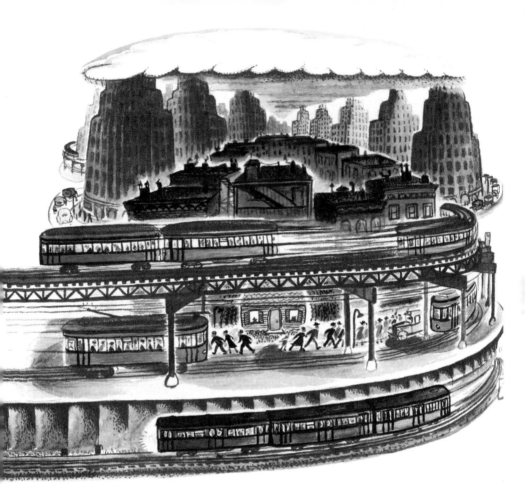

Pretty soon there was a subway
going back and forth underneath the Little House.
She couldn't see it, but she could feel and hear it.
People were moving faster and faster.
No one noticed the Little House any more.
They hurried by without a glance.

18

Pretty soon they tore down the apartment houses
and tenement houses around the Little House
and started digging big cellars . . . one on each side.
The steam shovels dug down three stories
on one side and four stories on the other side.
Pretty soon they started building up . . .
They built up twenty-five stories on one side
and thirty-five stories on the other.

19

Now the Little House
only saw the sun at noon,
and didn't see the moon or stars at night at all
because the lights of the city were too bright.
She didn't like living in the city.
At night she used to dream of the country
and the field of daisies and the apple trees
dancing in the moonlight.
The Little House was very sad and lonely.
Her paint was cracked and dirty . . .
Her windows were broken and her shutters
hung crookedly. She looked shabby . . .
though she was just as good
a house as ever underneath.

20

Then one fine morning in Spring along came
the great-great-granddaughter of the man
who built the Little House so well.
She saw the shabby Little House, but she didn't hurry by.
There was something about the Little House that
made her stop and look again. She said to her husband,
"That Little House looks just like the Little House
my grandmother lived in when she was a little girl,
only *that* Little House was way out
in the country on a hill covered with daisies
and apple trees growing around."

21

They found out it was the very same house,
so they went to the Movers to see
if the Little House could be moved.
The Movers looked the Little House all over
and said, "Sure, this house is as good as ever.
She's built so well we could move her anywhere."
So they jacked up the Little House
and put her on wheels.
Traffic was held up for hours
as they slowly moved her out of the city.

23

24

At first
the Little House
was frightened,
but after she got used to it
she rather liked it.
They rolled along the big road,
and they rolled along the little roads,
until they were way out in the country.
When the Little House saw the green
grass and heard the birds singing,
she didn't feel sad any more.
They went along and along,
but they couldn't seem to find
just the right place.
They tried the Little House here,
and they tried her there.

Finally they saw a little hill
in the middle of a field . . .
and apple trees growing around.
"There," said the
great-great-granddaughter,
"that's just the place."
"Yes, it is," said the Little House to herself.
A cellar was dug on top of the hill
and slowly they moved the house
from the road to the hill.

The windows and shutters were fixed
and once again they painted her
a lovely shade of pink.
As the Little House settled down
on her new foundation,
she smiled happily.
Once again she could watch
the sun and moon and stars.
Once again she could watch
Spring and Summer
and Fall and Winter
come and go.

Once again
  she was lived in
    and taken care of.

Never again would she be curious about the city . . .

Never again would she want to live there . . .

The stars twinkled above her . . .

A new moon was coming up . . .

It was Spring . . .

and all was quiet and peaceful in the country.

FOUR SEASONS MAKE A YEAR

ANNE ROCKWELL
PICTURES BY MEGAN HALSEY

A year has four seasons—
spring, summer, fall, and winter.
March twenty-first
is the first day of spring.
Wind blows and birds sing.
Daffodils and crocuses
pop up through melting snow
to bloom in the dark, wet earth.
Leaves sprout on the trees.
It's time to plow the field.

30

31

32

Spring showers come.
The pear tree we planted
by the porch is covered
with white blossoms.
A robin sings as it hunts
for worms in the ground.
It's time to plant corn and
squash seeds in the field.
I plant one sunflower seed
by the back door.

33

Breezes blow blossoms
from the pear tree into the sky.
Birds sing as they build nests.
Every day the air gets warmer.
The earth gets warmer, too.

34

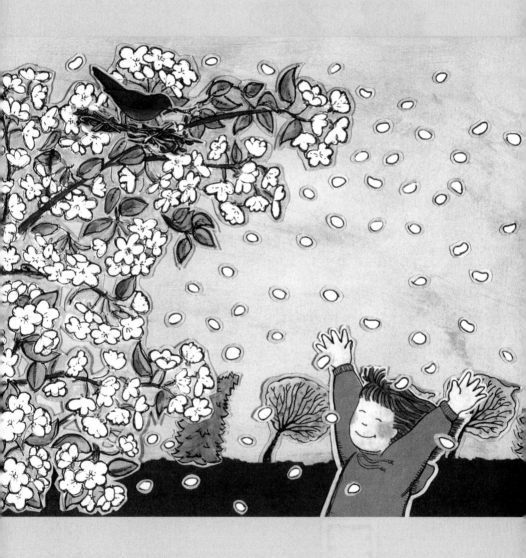

June twenty-first
is the first day of summer.
Green sprouts spring up
from the field.
My sunflower seed
sprouts green leaves, too.
Soon all the trees
are covered with leaves.
Roses bloom.
Bees buzz and butterflies
flutter among the flowers.
The pear tree's empty blossoms
turn to tiny green pears.

38

The flowerbed
in the front yard
bursts into bloom—
zinnias, sweet peas,
lilies, cosmos, and
black-eyed Susans.
The fields have
stalks of corn, along
with vines of green
pumpkins and squash.
On hot summer days
I swim in the pond
down the road.

40

Summer is when we
pick the first ears of
corn from the field.
We sell corn, squash,
and bouquets
of summer flowers
at our roadside stand.
But I won't sell my
big yellow-and-brown
sunflower, which has
grown so much
it's taller than I am!

41

September twenty-first
is the first day of fall.
Our pumpkins turn
from green to orange,
and I ride to school
on a big yellow bus.
My sunflower
droops its huge blossom,
heavy with seeds.

42

43

Leaves on the trees
turn red and gold.
Now I sleep
under a blanket
and wear a warm jacket
to school.
The bees and
butterflies are gone.
Many birds
fly away, too.

46

We pick the big
orange pumpkins
that grow in the field.
People drive out from
the city to buy them
at our roadside stand.
Cold wind makes
bright-colored leaves
dance through the air.

Corn stalks standing
in the field
turn dry and brown.
Pumpkin and squash
vines shrivel up.
It's time for the field
to rest.
Pears hanging
from the pear tree
are big and golden.
I bite into one that's
ripe, sweet, and juicy.

49

Now the sky
is gray and cold.
All the trees but
the evergreens
have bare branches.
Squirrels rush
frantically here and
there, hiding acorns
and nuts to eat
when winter comes.
Most of the birds
have flown away.

50

51

On December twenty-first
the first day of winter comes.
That very night,
snow starts to fall.
We sit by the fire
Papa built.
We watch flames
leap and glow
and listen to logs crackle.
Outside the snowflakes
fall thicker and faster.
They're still twirling white
in the black night
when it's time for me
to go to bed.

53

In the morning the
radio announcer says,
"No school today!"
The roads are slippery,
too covered with snow
for the big yellow bus
to travel safely.
A bright red cardinal
hops onto a snowbank.
Its mate comes to join it.
I think they're waiting
for me—for I know
just what they want.
Those birds love
sunflower seeds!

55

The big dried-up sunflower
I planted and grew and
saved is lying in a basket
in the mudroom.
I put on my snowsuit,
scarf, and mittens and
boots and go outside
in our cold white yard.
Deep snow comes to my
knees as I toss sunflower
seeds to the hungry
cardinals. Chickadees
come to eat them, too.

57

Under the blanket
of snow, everything
that grows in the
earth is having a
long winter rest.
But I'm not!
I'm building a bright
white snowman.
As I build, birds peck.
Soon all the sunflower
seeds are gone.
When spring comes
again, I'd better plant
two sunflower seeds
by our back door!

58

Houses

by Aileen Fisher

Houses are faces
(haven't you found?)
with their hats in the air,
and their necks in the ground.

Windows are noses,
windows are eyes,
and doors are the mouths
of a suitable size.

And a porch—or the place
where porches begin—
is just like a mustache
shading the chin.

Seasons of the Year

by Meish Goldish
(sung to "Here We Go Round the Mulberry Bush")

CHORUS:
Here we go round the year again,
The year again, the year again.
Here we go round the year again,
To greet the different seasons.

Wintertime is time for snow.
To the south, the birds will go.
It's too cold for plants to grow
Because it is the winter.

CHORUS

In the springtime, days grow warm.
On the plants, the new buds form.
Bees and bugs come out to swarm
Because it is the spring.

CHORUS

In summertime, the days are hot.
Ice cold drinks I drink a lot!
At the beach, I've got a spot
Because it is the summer.

CHORUS

Fall is here, the air is cool.
Days are short, it's back to school.
Raking leaves is now the rule
Because it is the autumn.

CHORUS

Grandpa's Stories

by Langston Hughes

The pictures on the television
Do not make me dream as well
As the stories without pictures
Grandpa knows how to tell.

Even if he does not know
What makes a Spaceman go,
Grandpa says back in his time
Hamburgers only cost a dime,
Ice cream cones a nickel,
And a penny for a pickle.

Children of Long Ago

by Lessie Jones Little

The children who lived a long time ago
In little country towns
Ate picnics under spreading trees,
Played hopscotch on the cool dirt yards,
Picked juicy grapes from broad grapevines,
Pulled beets and potatoes from the ground,
Those children of long ago.

The children who lived a long time ago
In little country towns
Tromped to school on hard-frozen roads,
Warmed themselves by wood-burning stoves,
Ate supper by light from oil-filled lamps,
Built fancy snowmen dressed like clowns,
Those children of long ago.

The children who lived a long time ago
In little country towns
Decked themselves in their Sunday best,
Went to church and visited friends,
Sang happy songs with their mamas and papas,
Traveled through books for sights and sounds,
Those children of long ago.

UNIT 2 • ACKNOWLEDGMENTS

Text

Excerpted from *The Little House,* by Virginia Lee Burton. Copyright © 1942 by Virginia Lee Burton, renewed 1969 by Aristides Burton Demetrios and Michael Burton Demetrios. Used by permission of Houghton Mifflin Harcourt Publishing Company. All rights reserved. Audio used with permission of Audible, Inc.

Four Seasons Make a Year, by Anne Rockwell, illustrations by Megan Halsey. Text copyright © 2004 by Anne Rockwell. Illustrations copyright © 2004 by Megan Halsey. Reprinted by permission of Walker & Co. All rights reserved.

"Houses," from *Up the Windy Hill* by Aileen Fisher. Copyright © 1953, renewed 1981 by Aileen Fisher. All rights reserved. Used by permission of Marian Reiner on behalf of the Boulder Public Library Foundation, Inc.

"Seasons of the Year," from *101 Science Poems and Songs for Young Learners* by Meish Goldish. Copyright © 1996 by Meish Goldish. Reprinted by permission of Scholastic Inc.

"Grandpa's Stories," from *The Collected Poems of Langston Hughes* by Langston Hughes, edited by Arnold Rampersad with David Roessel, Associate Editor. Copyright © 1994 by the Estate of Langston Hughes. Used by permission of Harold Ober Associates Incorporated and by permission of Alfred A. Knopf, an imprint of the Knopf Doubleday Publishing Group, a division of Random House LLC. All rights reserved. Any third party use of this material, outside of this publication, is prohibited. Interested parties must apply directly to Random House LLC for permission.

"Children of Long Ago," from *Children of Long Ago* by Lessie Jones Little. Copyright © 2000 by Lessie Jones Little. Permission arranged with Lee & Low Books, Inc., New York, NY 10016. All rights not specifically granted herein are reserved.

Illustrations
60 Shelly Hehenberger, **61** Ian Joven, **62** Kristin Sorra, **63** Gynux

64